SEASON & SPICE™
And Everything Nice!

*The Ultimate Dry Rub, Paste
& Basting Cookbook*

SEASON & SPICE™
And Everything Nice!

The Ultimate Dry Rub, Paste & Basting Cookbook

Printed in China
Copyright © 2013 KitchenAdvance
ISBN: 978-1-938653-14-8

Table of Contents

Pastes

Basting Sauces   89

Dry Rubs

Dry rubs are often referred to as a "spice rub" as they are made from a combination of ground spices that is rubbed on and into raw meats or fish before cooking. Acting as a coating on the meat or fish, one can either cook with the rub immediately, or allow it to marinate into the food to better season and infuse the flavors. Generally made with coarsely ground spices, sugar is often used if one wants a sweeter rub, or for caramelization.

Rubs are quite different all around the world, but their varying ingredients are entirely up to the cook. While we have gathered many variations of combinations that will keep any herb and spice lover happy for years to come, many rubs you have or will taste are secret recipes to that culture or cook, and so we encourage each cook to try creating his or her own personal rub after understanding how simple they truly are.

Dry rubs are often made with ground herbs, and while they don't spoil, they do lose their potency. Therefore, although they can be used past the suggested storage time, the mixtures will be less flavorful.

Asian Dry Rub

2 tbsp *anise seeds*
2 tsp *fennel seeds*
2 tsp *szechuan peppers, ground*
½ tsp *cloves, whole*
1 tsp *red pepper flakes*
1 stick *cinnamon*
1 tbsp *black peppercorns*
1 tsp *salt*
2 tsp *brown sugar*
2 tsp *ground ginger*

yields: ½ cup

Grind anise, fennel, cloves, cinnamon stick, and peppercorns in mortar and pestle or spice grinder, and then combine with dry ingredients.

SUGGESTED USE

pork roast (1 hour)
chicken (1 hour)

Barbecue Rub

¼ cup *paprika*
1 tbsp *ground cumin*
1 tbsp *brown sugar*
1 tbsp *chili powder*
1 tsp *garlic powder*
1 tsp *salt*
½ tsp *cayenne pepper*
½ tsp *freshly ground pepper*

yields: ¾ cup

Combine all ingredients and store in a jar for up to 6-8 months.

SUGGESTED USE

ribs (6 to 8 hours)
pork loin or tenderloin (3 to 4 hours)
whole chicken or chicken pieces
(2 to 3 hours)

Bayou Pork Rub

5 tbsp *salt*
5 tbsp *paprika*
10 tbsp *brown sugar*
2 tbsp *ground dried thyme*
2 tbsp *dried oregano*
2 tbsp *dried basil*
2 tbsp *ground black pepper*
10 tbsp *garlic powder*
10 tbsp *onion powder*
1 tbsp *cayenne pepper*
1 tbsp *ground cloves*
1 tbsp *ground allspice*
1 tbsp *ground mustard*

yields: 3½ cup

Combine all ingredients in a medium bowl, and mix evenly.

SUGGESTED USE

pork butt, ribs or brisket (24 hours)

Big Spice Texas Rub

6 tbsp *paprika*
2 tbsp *ground black pepper*
2 tbsp *chili powder*
2 tbsp *salt*
2 tbsp *sugar*
1 tbsp *garlic powder*
1 tbsp *onion powder*
1½ tsp *cayenne pepper*

yields: ¾ cup

Combine all ingredients and store in a jar for up to 6-8 months.

SUGGESTED USE

beef steak (1 hour)
beef roast (4 to 6 hours)
pork loin or tenderloin (2 to 3 hours)
spareribs (6 to 8 hours)
whole chicken (2 hours)
chicken breasts (1 hour)

Brown Sugar Cumin Rub

½ cup *golden brown sugar*
2½ tbsp *ground cumin*
1 tbsp *kosher salt*
½ tsp *cayenne pepper*

yields: ⅔ cup

Place all ingredients in a small bowl and mix together thoroughly.

SUGGESTED USE

pork chops, tenderloin, or loin
(30 minutes)
pork butt or roast (1 hour)

Cajun Creole Rub

2 tbsp *paprika*
1 tbsp *garlic powder*
2 tsp *dried thyme*
½ tsp *dried oregano*
1 tsp *cayenne pepper*
1 tsp *salt*
1 tsp *freshly ground pepper*

yields: ½ cup

Combine all ingredients and store in a jar for up to 6-8 months.

SUGGESTED USE

whole chicken or chicken pieces
(2 hours)
pork loin, tenderloin, or chops
(2 hours)
fish (30 minutes)

Carolina Barbecue Rub

2 tbsp *ground cumin*
2 tbsp *chili powder*
1 tbsp *cayenne pepper*
¼ cup *paprika*
2 tbsp *sugar*
2 tbsp *brown sugar*
2 tbsp *black pepper, freshly ground*
2 tbsp *salt*

yields: 1 cup

Combine all ingredients in a small bowl and mix well. Store in a jar for up to 6-8 months.

SUGGESTED USE

whole chicken or chicken pieces
(2 hours)
pork loin, tenderloin, or chops
(2 hours)
lamb (2 hours)
beef (1-2 hours)

Chipotle Cocoa Mole Rub

¼ cup *sea salt*
2 tsp *unsweetened cocoa powder*
2 tsp *chipotle chili power*
3 tbsp *dark brown sugar*
2 tbsp *garlic powder*
1 tbsp *onion powder*
3 tbsp *ground cumin*
3 tbsp *ground cinnamon*
1 tsp *ground cloves*
2 tbsp *freshly ground black pepper*

yields: 1 cup

Combine all ingredients in a medium bowl, and mix evenly.

SUGGESTED USE

beef (2 hours)
pork (1 hour)
chicken (30 minutes

Fiery Red Pepper Rub

2 tbsp *paprika*
1 tbsp *cayenne pepper*
1 tbsp *garlic powder*
1 tbsp *onion powder*
1 tsp *dried thyme*
1 tsp *dried oregano*
2 tsp *freshly ground pepper*
1 tbsp *kosher salt*

yields: ½ cup

Place all ingredients into a small bowl. Stir well to combine. Store airtight in a jar for up to 1 month, or 6 months in the freezer.

SUGGESTED USE

chicken wings (6 hours)
boneless chicken breast (30 minutes)
pork spareribs (6 hours)
pork chops (1 hour)

Four Peppercorn Rub

1 tbsp *black peppercorns*
1 tbsp *white peppercorns*
1 tbsp *green peppercorns*
1 tsp *pink peppercorns*
1 tbsp *salt*

yields: ¼ cup

In a spice grinder or mortar and pestle, grind peppercorns into a coarse mixture, and stir in the salt. Store in a jar for 1-2 months.

SUGGESTED USE

beef roast or steak (1 hour)
beef tenderloin (30 minutes)

Garam Masala Rub

1½ tbsp *ground cardamom*
1½ tbsp *ground cinnamon*
2 tbsp *ground cloves*
2 tbsp *ground black pepper*
1 tsp *ground cumin*
¾ tsp *ground coriander*
¼ tsp *ground nutmeg*
2 tsp *salt*

yields: ½ cup

Place cardamom, cinnamon, cloves, pepper, cumin and coriander in a small skillet over a medium low heat. Toast spices, tossing often until they begin to perfume the air. Stir in the nutmeg and salt; let cool completely. Keep in a jar for 3-4 months.

SUGGESTED USE

whole chicken (30 minutes)
pork loin (1 hour)

Garlic & Paprika Rub

1 tbsp *paprika*
1 tsp *dry mustard*
1 clove *garlic, finely chopped*
to taste *salt & black pepper*

yields: 2 tbsp

Combine all ingredients in a medium bowl, and mix evenly.
Use immediately.

SUGGESTED USE

chicken wings (4 to 6 hours)

Ginger & Garlic Rub

2 tbsp *onion powder*
2 tbsp *garlic powder*
2 tbsp *ground ginger*
2 tsp *ground black pepper*
½ tsp *salt*

yields: ¼ cup

Combine all ingredients in a medium bowl, and mix evenly.

SUGGESTED USE

Try this with chicken, turkey, or pork.

Herbed Pepper Rub

2 tbsp *paprika*
1 tsp *dried thyme*
1 tsp *dried oregano*
1 tsp *freshly ground white pepper*
1 tsp *freshly ground black pepper*
½ tsp *cayenne pepper*
1 tbsp *salt*
1 tbsp *garlic powder*
1 tbsp *onion powder*

yields: ½ cup

*Toss ingredients together in a small bowl. Store in a jar
for 6-8 months.*

SUGGESTED USE

beef roast (4 hours)
chicken wings (4 to 6 hours)
kabobs (2 hours)

*Try tossing this mixture with onions and
vegetables.*

Indian Curry Rub

3 tbsp *ground coriander*
2 tbsp *ground cumin*
2 tsp *freshly ground pepper*
2 tsp *ground cloves*
2 tsp *ground cinnamon*
2 tsp *ground ginger*
2 tsp *ground cardamom*
1 tsp *ground cayenne*
2 tbsp *ground turmeric*
1 tbsp *salt*

yields: 1¼ cup

Place coriander, cumin, pepper, cloves, cinnamon, ginger and cardamom in a small skillet over medium low heat. Toast spices, tossing often, until they begin to perfume the air. Stir in the cayenne, turmeric and salt. Keep in a jar for 3-4 months.

SUGGESTED USE

chicken pieces (30 minutes)
pork tenderloin (30 to 60 minutes)
beef steak (20 minutes)

Italian Herb Rub

2 tbsp *dried basil, finely crumbled*
2 tbsp *dried oregano, finely crumbled*
1 tbsp *dried thyme, finely crumbled*
1 tbsp *dried rosemary, finely crumbled*
1 tbsp *dried sage, finely crumbled*
1 tbsp *salt*
1 tsp *freshly ground pepper*

yields: ½ cup

Combine all ingredients and store in a jar for up to 6-8 months.

SUGGESTED USE

chicken (2 hours)
fish fillets (1 hour)

This mixture can also be used as a seasoning for spaghetti sauce.

Orange Chipotle Rub

2 tbsp *orange zest, air-dried for an hour*
2 tbsp *ancho chili powder*
2 tbsp *chili powder*
1 tbsp *chipotle chili powder or crushed dried chipotle peppers*
1 tsp *ground cumin*
1 tsp *dried oregano*
1 tsp *salt*

yields: ¼ cup

Place dried zest in a small bowl with other ingredients and toss to combine well. Store in freezer for up to 2 months.

SUGGESTED USE

beef sirloin (1 hour)
beef kabobs (1 hour)
pork (1 hour)

Rosemary Pepper Rub

¼ cup *rosemary, chopped*
1 tbsp *black pepper, coarsely ground*
1 tsp *dry mustard*
1 tsp *dried oregano*
1 tsp *garlic powder*
2 tsp *kosher salt*

yields: ½ cup

With a mortar and pestle, spice grinder or blender, grind ingredients to a coarse powder. Keeps tightly sealed in the freezer for 3 months.

SUGGESTED USE

lamb chops or butterflied leg of lamb
(2 hours)
whole chicken, or chicken pieces
(2 hours)

Savory Dried Herb Rub

2 tbsp *dried crumbled basil*
1 tbsp *dried thyme*
1 tbsp *dried rubbed sage*
1 tbsp *garlic powder*
2 tsp *dried crumbled rosemary*
1 tsp *dried oregano*
1 tsp *salt*
¼ tsp *freshly ground pepper*

yields: ⅓ cup

Combine all the ingredients in a mortar and pestle or a spice grinder and blend together. Store in a jar for up to 6-8 months.

SUGGESTED USE

pork chops, loin, or tenderloin
(1 hour)
whole turkey or breast (1 hour)
whole chicken or breast (1 hour)

Dill Mustard Spice Rub

1 tbsp *ground black pepper*
1 tbsp *ground white pepper*
1 tbsp *salt*
1½ tsp *celery seeds*
1½ tsp *dried thyme*
1½ tsp *dill seeds*
1½ tsp *mustard seeds*
1½ tsp *garlic powder*
½ tsp *dried red pepper flakes*

yields: ½ cup

Combine all ingredients in a blender, mini-processor, spice grinder or mortar and pestle and blend well. Store in a jar for 2-3 months.

SUGGESTED USE

chicken pieces (30 minutes)
lamb chops or butterflied leg of lamb
(30 to 60 minutes)

Toasted Fennel Rub

1 cup *fennel seeds*
3 tbsp *coriander seeds*
2 tbsp *white peppercorns*
3 tbsp *kosher salt*

yields: 1¼ cup

Put all but the salt into a heavy pan over medium heat. Toss frequently to toast evenly. When fragrant and light brown, remove from heat and cool completely. Put into a food processor and add salt. Process to a fine powder. Store in a jar for up to 6-8 months.

SUGGESTED USE

pork chops, ribs or tenderloin
(1 hour)
beef (1 hour)
roast vegetables (30 minutes)

Tropical Sweet Spice Rub

1 tbsp *ground allspice*
1 tbsp *ground nutmeg*
1 tbsp *ground cinnamon*
1 tsp *ground cloves*
1 tsp *cayenne pepper*
1 tsp *salt*

yields: ½ cup

Combine all ingredients and store in a jar for up to 3-5 months.

SUGGESTED USE

shrimp (30 minutes)
fish fillets (30 minutes)
boneless chicken breasts (30 minutes)

Pestos

Pesto originated in Genoa in the Liguria region of Italy. In its history, the word means to pound or to crush. As far back as ancient Rome, pesto has existed in various forms and names. Today's definition of pesto was first written about by Giovanni Battista Ratto in the 1863 book, *La Cuciniera Genovese*.

Today the term pesto is used quite loosely. Within this book we have given the original recipe, *Pesto alla genovese*, but we also have included quite a few inventive variations.

In today's markets, there are many pre-made forms of pesto that can be purchased, but within this book we have gathered some of our very favorites, and once you taste how delicious a homemade pesto is on pasta, you will never buy it from a can again.

Arugula Pesto

3 to 4 cloves *garlic, peeled & sliced*
½ cup *olive oil*
3 cups *arugula*
½ cup *Parmesan cheese, freshly grated*
½ cup *garbanzo beans from a can, drained and rinsed*
to taste *lemon juice, freshly squeezed*

yields: 2 cup

*In a small skillet, heat a small amount of olive oil over medium heat.
Add the garlic, and cook for 1 to 3 minutes until the garlic begins
to turn golden. Let cool. Into a food processor, combine the garlic,
arugula, Parmesan, garbanzo beans, and lemon juice, and process
until finely chopped. With the machine running, add the oil in a steady
stream. Use immediately or cover tightly and refrigerate for 1-2 weeks.*

SUGGESTED USE

*This pesto is great mixed in with pasta, boiled
or roasted potatoes or other root vegetables.*

Basil Parsley Pesto

2 cloves *garlic, peeled*
1 cup *basil*
½ cup *Italian or flat-leaf parsley*
3 tbsp *pine nuts*
3 tbsp *Parmesan, grated*
½ tsp *salt*
½ cup *olive oil*

yields: ½ cup

With the food processor running, drop in the garlic cloves and process until minced. Turn off the machine and add the basil, parsley, pine nuts, Parmesan and salt. Pulse to finely chop the ingredients. With the machine running again, pour in the oil and process to make a paste. Use immediately or cover tightly and refrigerate for up to 5 days or freeze for up to 3 months.

SUGGESTED USE

whole chicken, rubbed under & over the skin (2 hours)
chicken pieces or boneless breasts (2 hours)

This pesto is very close to the original recipe but adds parsley. It is fantastic with pasta.

Celery Leaf Pesto

2 cups *celery leaves/tops*
⅓ cup *almonds, blanched*
3 cloves *garlic*
⅓ cup *Parmesan, freshly grated*
¾ cup *olive oil*
1 tsp *salt*

yields: 3 cups

In a food processor add celery leaves, almonds, garlic, and Parmesan and pulse a few times. With the machine running, add the oil in a steady stream. Add salt and mix well by hand. Use immediately or cover tightly and refrigerate for 1-2 weeks.

SUGGESTED USE

whole chicken, rubbed under & over the skin (2 hours)
chicken pieces or boneless breasts (2 hours)

This pesto is also fantastic with pasta.

Chard Pesto

½ cup *walnuts*
1½ oz *Parmesan, freshly grated*
4 cloves *garlic*
¾ tsp *salt*
1½ cups *chard leaves, packed*
¾ cup *basil*
¼ cup *olive oil*

yields: 1 cup

In a food processor add walnuts, Parmesan, garlic, and salt and pulse a few times. Then add chard and basil, and pulse until combined. With the machine running, add the oil in a steady stream. Use immediately or cover tightly and refrigerate for 1-2 weeks.

SUGGESTED USE

chicken pieces or boneless breasts
(2 hours)

Try this as a sauce for grilled meat. This pesto is also fantastic with pasta.

Chili Pesto

¼ cup *red onion, chopped*
1 large clove *garlic, minced*
4 dried *New Mexico chiles, stemmed & seeded*
¼ cup *olive oil*
¾ cup *water*
¼ cup *pepitas (pumpkin seeds)*
1 tsp *thyme*
½ tsp *ground cumin*
½ tsp *salt*

yields: 1 cup

Over medium heat, toast pepitas in a skillet. Stir 2 to 4 minutes, until fragrant and lightly browned. Heat olive oil in a large skillet over medium heat. Add onion and cook, stirring often, until soft, 2 minutes. Add garlic, chiles and cook about a minute. Add water and turn off the heat. Pour the mixture into a bowl and cover. Set aside to soften, about 20 minutes. Pour the mixture into a food processor with pepitas, thyme, cumin and salt. Pulse a few times, then process until smooth.

SUGGESTED USE

This pesto is fantastic with grilled vegetables, and meats.

Cilantro Pesto

2 cups *cilantro, packed*
½ cup *almonds, blanched*
¼ cup *red onion, chopped*
½ tsp *serrano chile, chopped & seeded*
1 tsp *salt*
¼ cup *olive oil*

yields: 1 cup

In a food processor add cilantro, almonds, onion, chile, and salt, and pulse a few times. With the machine running, add the oil in a steady stream. Use immediately or cover tightly and refrigerate for 1-2 weeks.

SUGGESTED USE

chicken (1 hour)
shrimp (30 minutes)

For a spicier pesto, add more of the serrano chile.

Goat Cheese Parsley Pesto

4 oz *soft goat cheese, crumbled*
1 cup *flat-leaf parsley leaves, packed*
½ cup *fresh oregano leaves (about 1 bunch), packed*
2 tbsp *water*
1 tsp *Dijon mustard*
½ tsp *pepper, freshly ground*
¼ tsp *salt*

yields: 1 cup

In a food processor, add all ingredients, and pulse a few times. Then process until smooth. Use immediately or cover tightly and refrigerate for 1-2 weeks.

SUGGESTED USE

This pesto is great as a topping on chicken or fish, or as dip for an appetizer, or mixed with a pasta.

Kale & Walnut Pesto

⅓ cup *walnuts*
12 cups *kale, cut leaves from thick inner stems, and tear*
1 cup *pecorino, grated*
1 clove *garlic*
½ tsp *salt*
¼ tsp *black pepper*
½ cup *olive oil*

yields: 2 cups

Toast the walnuts in a 350° F oven, tossing occasionally, for about 5-8 minutes, or until they become fragrant. In a large pot of boiling salted water, cook the kale for about 30 seconds, or until bright green. Drain and pat dry. In a food processor, combine the kale, pecorino, garlic, walnuts, salt, and pepper, and process until finely chopped. With the machine running, add the oil in a steady stream. Use immediately or cover tightly and refrigerate for 1-2 weeks.

SUGGESTED USE

chicken pieces (2 hours)
grilled salmon, with pesto spooned over

This pesto is also fantastic with pasta.

Italian Parsley Pesto

3 cloves *garlic, peeled*
1 cup *Italian or flat-leaf parsley*
½ tsp *lemon zest*
¼ cup *pine nuts*
¼ cup *Parmesan, grated*
¼ tsp *salt*
⅓ cup *olive oil*

yields: ¾ cup

Mince the garlic in a food processor. Turn off the machine and add the parsley, lemon zest, pine nuts, Parmesan and salt. Pulse to finely chop the ingredients. With the machine running again, pour in the oil and process to make a paste. Use immediately or cover tightly and refrigerate for up to 5 days or freeze for up to 3 months.

SUGGESTED USE

fish fillet (30 minutes)
skewered shrimp (1 hour)

Mint Pesto

2 cloves *garlic, peeled*
½ cup *mint*
¼ cup *basil*
1 cup *Italian or flat-leaf parsley*
⅓ cup *pine nuts*
½ tsp *salt*
½ cup *olive oil*

yields: 1½ cup

With the food processor running, drop in the garlic and process until minced. Turn off the machine and add the mint, basil, parsley, pine nuts and salt. Pulse to finely chop the ingredients. With the machine running again, pour in the oil and process to make a paste. Use immediately or cover tightly and refrigerate for up to 3 days or freeze for up to 1 month.

SUGGESTED USE

leg of lamb (6 hours)
lamb chops (2 hours)

Pesto alla Genovese

3 cups *basil leaves, washed*
2 cloves *garlic*
½ cup *pine nuts*
coarse sea salt
⅔ cup *olive oil (preferably Ligurian)*
¼ cup *Parmesan, freshly grated*
¼ cup *Pecorino Romano, freshly grated*

yields: 2 cups

Put the garlic in the mortar, then add the basil with a dash of sea salt. Gently roll the pestle against the mortar walls, shredding the basil leaves as you go, until juice from the basil appears. Add the pine nuts and crush. Then add the cheeses and continue to stir until paste is formed. While slowly rolling the pestle, slowly add the olive oil.

SUGGESTED USE

This is the classic pesto recipe. High quality ingredients are very important. The basil must be young (small leaves & fragrant). Pesto can be stored with olive oil on top in a jar for 1-2 weeks in the refrigerator.

Pistachio Pesto

1½ cups *basil, packed*
1 cup *olive oil*
1 cup *pistachios, dry-roasted*
½ cup *cilantro, packed*
¼ cup *Parmesan, finely grated*
1 tsp *lemon zest*
3 cloves *garlic*
to taste *salt & black pepper, freshly ground*

yields: 1¼ cup

In a food processor, add all ingredients, and pulse a few times. Then process until smooth. Use immediately or cover tightly and refrigerate for 1-2 weeks.

SUGGESTED USE

This pesto is great mixed with pasta, roast vegetables, or even just spread on toast.

Pistou

½ cup *fresh basil*
6 small cloves *garlic, quartered*
1 cup *Parmesan, finely grated*
⅔ cup *olive oil*
¼ tsp *salt*
⅛ tsp *black pepper, ground*

yields: 1¼ cup

In a mortar and pestle, pound the ingredients until smooth. Or in a food processor, add all ingredients, and process until smooth. Use immediately or cover tightly and refrigerate for 1-2 weeks.

SUGGESTED USE

Pistou is from French Provence, and evolved from the classic Italian pesto recipe, eliminating pine nuts. It is used on pasta, bread, or in the Provençal Soupe au Pistou.

Radish Leaf Pesto

4 cups *radish leaves*
1 clove *garlic, mashed*
¼ cup *almonds, toasted*
½ cup *Parmesan, freshly grated*
1 tbsp *lemon juice*
⅓ cup *olive oil*
to taste *salt & black pepper, freshly ground*

yields: 1½ cup

In a food processor add radish leaves, garlic, almonds, Parmesan and lemon juice and pulse a few times. With the machine running, add the oil in a steady stream. Add salt and pepper and mix well by hand. Use immediately or cover tightly and refrigerate for 1-2 weeks.

SUGGESTED USE

This pesto is great with pasta, on toast as an appetizer, or even on a sandwich.

Ramp Pesto

⅔ cup *walnuts, chopped*
½ cup *olive oil*
½ cup *Parmesan, freshly grated*
1 small bunch *parsley*
1 small bunch *ramps*
to taste *salt*

yields: 1⅓ cup

Toast walnuts in a frying pan over medium heat, tossing occasionally, until fragrant, about 5-7 minutes. In a large pot of boiling salted water, blanch the parsley for about 30 seconds to 1 minute, or until bright green. Fill a large bowl with ice water, then submerge parsley in the ice water. Cut off the leaves of the ramps, and repeat above with ramp leaves. Drain and dry the parsley and ramp leaves well. Chop well and put into food processor with walnuts, Parmesan and salt. Pulse a few times, then, with the motor running, drizzle in the olive oil slowly until the oil is incorporated. Use immediately or cover and refrigerate up to 2 days.

SUGGESTED USE

This pesto is great mixed with pasta, roast vegetables, or even just spread on toast.

Spinach Pesto

½ cup *basil*
1½ cups *spinach*
4 cloves *garlic, minced*
½ cup *olive oil*
½ cup *Parmesan, freshly grated*
⅓ cup *pine nuts*
to taste *salt & pepper*

yields: 1 cup

In a food processor, add all ingredients, and pulse a few times. Then process until smooth. Use immediately or cover tightly and refrigerate for 1-2 weeks.

SUGGESTED USE

This pesto is great with pasta, roast vegetables, or even on a sandwich.

Sun-Dried Tomato Pesto

2 heads *garlic*
2 oz *sun-dried tomatoes*
2 cups *water*
¼ cup *Asiago cheese, grated*
2 tsp *fresh oregano leaves, packed*
2 tbsp *olive oil*
1 tsp *red-wine vinegar*
¼ tsp *crushed red pepper*
¼ tsp *salt*

yields: 1 cup

Slice top off garlic, exposing the inner cloves. In foil, roast until soft, about 45 minutes. Let cool, then remove the cloves from the skin. Place tomatoes in a bowl, cover with boiling water and let soak until soft, about 20 minutes. Remove from water. In a food processor pulse the tomatoes, 6 tablespoons of the boiling water, cheese, oregano, oil, vinegar, red pepper, salt, and roasted garlic cloves. Process until smooth. Use immediately or cover tightly and refrigerate for 1-2 weeks.

SUGGESTED USE

This pesto is wonderful with chicken, pasta, or halibut.

Tarragon Pesto

2 cloves *garlic, peeled*
½ cup *tarragon*
1 cup *Italian or flat-leaf parsley*
¼ cup *walnuts, chopped*
¼ cup *Parmesan, grated*
to taste *salt*
⅓ cup *olive oil*

yields: 1 cup

With the food processor running, drop in the garlic cloves and process until minced. Turn off the machine and add the tarragon, parsley, walnuts, Parmesan and salt. Pulse to finely chop the ingredients. With the machine running again, pour in the oil and process to make a paste. Use immediately or cover tightly and refrigerate for up to 3 days or freeze for up to 1 month.

SUGGESTED USE

whole chicken, rubbed under & over the skin (2 hours)
chicken pieces or boneless breasts (1 hour)

This pesto also works well tossed with cooked vegetables.

Pastes

Pastes are any combination of ingredients pounded until they become a smooth or semi smooth creamy mass. While it is possible to include pesto with pastes, it is because pesto has such a unique definition that we gave it its own section.

Pastes are often made from spicy and aromatic flavors. Used as a spread for an appetizer, or a condiment on the side, pastes are a great addition to a dish. They are also used to coat other foods when cooking, or as a starter or basis for a more complex dish or sauce.

In this section we hope you find many interesting and surprising combinations that will become additions and staples in your home cooking.

Asian Sesame Chili Paste

2 cloves *garlic, minced*
1 tsp *orange zest*
1 to 2 tsp *red pepper flakes*
½ tsp *ground coriander*
¼ cup *hoisin sauce*
1 tbsp *sesame oil*
1 tbsp *soy sauce*
1 tbsp *vegetable oil*

yields: ⅓ cup

In a small bowl mash together the garlic, orange zest, red pepper flakes and coriander. Stir in the hoisin, sesame oil, soy sauce and oil to make a paste. Use immediately or cover tightly and refrigerate up to 3 days.

SUGGESTED USE

shrimp (2 to 3 hours)
chicken (4 to 6 hours)
pork tenderloin (4 to 6 hours)

Caribbean Spice Paste

2 tbsp *vegetable oil*
2 tbsp *lime juice*
1 small *onion, chopped*
1½ tbsp *ginger, minced*
3 cloves *garlic, minced*
2 *jalapeño chilies, seeded & chopped*
2 tbsp *parsley, minced*
1 tbsp *dried thyme*
½ tsp *dry mustard*
½ tsp *salt*

yields: 1 cup

Combine ingredients in a food processor and purée. Use immediately or cover tightly and refrigerate up to 1 week.

SUGGESTED USE

chicken pieces (2 hours)
shrimp (30 minutes)
boneless leg of lamb (4 to 6 hours)

Charmoula Paste

½ cup *parsley, chopped*
½ cup *cilantro, chopped*
1 tbsp *ground cinnamon*
1 tbsp *ground ginger*
1 tbsp *paprika*
1 tsp *freshly ground pepper*
½ tsp *ground cumin*
½ tsp *ground thyme*
½ tsp *cayenne pepper*
½ tsp *salt*
1 tbsp *lemon juice*
¼ cup *olive oil*

yields: 1½ cup

Place parsley and cilantro in food processor and chop. Add cinnamon, ginger, paprika, pepper, cumin, thyme, cayenne and salt. Pulse to combine. Add lemon juice and olive oil and purée into a thick paste.

SUGGESTED USE

chicken breasts (1 hour)
shrimp (1 hour)
fish fillets (30 minutes)

Charmoula is used in Algerian, Moroccan and Tunisian cooking.

Chipotle Honey Paste

2 cloves *garlic, peeled*
¼ cup *onion, chopped*
3 *dried chipotle chilies*
3 tbsp *honey*
1 tbsp *lime juice*
½ tsp *salt*

yields: ¾ cup

Pour boiling water over dried chilies in a bowl. Let soak for 30 minutes. With a food processor running, drop in the garlic and process until finely minced. Add the onion and chilies. Pulse to finely chop. Add the honey, lime juice and salt, then purée. Use immediately or cover tightly and store in the refrigerator for up to 1 week.

SUGGESTED USE

steak (2 to 3 hours)
tuna steaks (2 hours)
chicken breasts (2 hours)

Garlic Rosemary Paste

¼ cup *rosemary*
4 cloves *garlic, minced*
½ tsp *dried oregano*
½ tsp *salt*
½ tsp *freshly ground pepper*
2 tbsp *olive oil*

yields: ½ cup

Combine rosemary, garlic, and oregano in a food processor and process until finely chopped. Add the salt, pepper and olive oil and process to a paste. Use immediately.

SUGGESTED USE

pork loin (4 to 6 hours)
pork tenderloin (3 to 4 hours)
boneless leg of lamb (8 hours)
chicken breasts (2 to 3 hours)
swordfish steaks (1 hour)

Hoisin Orange Paste

¼ cup *hoisin sauce*
3 tbsp *soy sauce*
1 tbsp *sesame oil*
2 tbsp *orange zest*
2 cloves *garlic, minced*
1 tsp *crushed red pepper flakes*
1 tsp *ground coriander*
½ tsp *ground cumin*
¼ cup *sesame seeds, toasted*

yields: ¾ cup

Place hoisin sauce, soy sauce, sesame oil, garlic and orange zest in a medium bowl. Stir well to combine. Stir in the red pepper flakes, coriander, cumin and sesame seeds. Keep covered in refrigerator up to 1 week.

SUGGESTED USE

chicken breasts (3 hours)
pork tenderloin (3 to 24 hours)
shrimp (2 hours)

Indian Curry Paste

4 cloves *garlic, minced*
½ cup *cilantro*
2 tbsp *curry powder*
¼ tsp *cayenne pepper (optional)*
½ tsp *salt*
¼ cup *cashew pieces*
¼ cup *lemon juice*
¼ cup *vegetable oil*

yields: 1 cup

With the food processor running drop in the garlic and process to finely mince. Turn off machine and add all but the oil. Pulse to mince and process to purée. With the machine running pour in the oil. Use immediately or cover tightly and refrigerate up to 1 week.

SUGGESTED USE

shrimp or scallops (2 hours)
chicken breasts (3 to 4 hours)
lamb kabobs (4 to 6 hours)

Italian Dried Herb Paste

6 cloves *garlic, minced*
2 tbsp *dried basil, finely crumbled*
2 tbsp *dried oregano, finely crumbled*
1 tbsp *dried thyme, finely crumbled*
1 tbsp *dried rosemary, finely crumbled*
1 tbsp *dried sage, finely crumbled*
½ tsp *salt*
½ tsp *freshly ground pepper*
⅓ cup *olive oil*

yields: 1 cup

Mash the garlic with the dried herbs, salt and pepper with a mortar and pestle to make a crumbly mixture. Mash in the olive oil. Use immediately or cover and refrigerate for up to 24 hours.

SUGGESTED USE

zucchini slices (15 minutes)
fish fillets (1 hour)
chicken breasts (3 hours)
whole chicken (4 hours)
lamb chops (3 hours)
leg of lamb (8 to 12 hours)

Jalapeño & Garlic Paste

1 clove *garlic, minced*
2 *jalapeño, minced*
2 tbsp *olive oil*

yields: ¼ cup

In a small bowl or with a mortar and pestle, mash the garlic and jalapeño. Mash in the oil to form a paste.

SUGGESTED USE

large shrimp (30 minutes)
boneless chicken breasts
(30 to 60 minutes)

Jamaican Jerk Paste

2 tbsp *cilantro, chopped*
1 tbsp *ginger, finely minced*
2 tbsp *lime juice*
2 tbsp *olive oil*
3 tbsp *golden brown sugar*
½ tsp *ground nutmeg*
½ tsp *cayenne pepper*
¼ tsp *ground allspice*
¼ tsp *ground cinnamon*
¼ tsp *salt*

yields: ¾ cup

Place cilantro, ginger, lime juice and olive oil in a medium bowl. Stir around to combine. Stir in remaining ingredients. Use immediately or cover and refrigerate up to 2 days.

SUGGESTED USE

pork loin (4 hours)
pork tenderloin (2 hours)
pork or lamb kabobs (1 to 3 hours)
boneless leg of lamb (8 hours)

Jerk Paste

1 bunch *green onions, chopped*
4 *Scotch bonnet chilies or*
10 *jalapeño chilies*
1 tbsp *ground allspice*
1 tsp *ground cinnamon*
¼ tsp *ground nutmeg*
2 tsp *salt*
⅓ cup *red wine vinegar*
2 tbsp *soy sauce*
2 tbsp *vegetable oil*
to taste *hot sauce*

yields: ⅔ cup

Place green onion and chilies in food processor or blender and process to chop. Add allspice, cinnamon, nutmeg, salt, vinegar, soy sauce and oil. Process to purée and liquefy. Add hot sauce to taste. Store covered tightly in the refrigerator up to 2 weeks.

SUGGESTED USE

chicken pieces (4 hours)
shrimp (2 hours)
pork chops (4 hours)
pork or chicken kabobs (2 hours)

Lemon Coriander Paste

1 tbsp *olive oil*
2 tsp *lemon juice*
1 tsp *Dijon mustard*
1 tsp *onion, minced*
1 tsp *garlic, minced*
1 tsp *paprika*
½ tsp *ground coriander*
½ tsp *freshly ground white pepper*

yields: ¼ cup

Place oil in a small bowl. Whisk in the remaining ingredients.

SUGGESTED USE

boneless chicken breasts (30 minutes)
pork tenderloin (60 minutes)
shark or swordfish (20 to 30 minutes)

Lemon Herb Paste

5 cloves *garlic, minced*
1 tbsp *lemon zest*
1 tbsp *dried thyme, crumbled*
2 tbsp *rosemary, crumbled*
2 tsp *dried sage leaves, crumbled*
½ tsp *salt*
¼ tsp *freshly ground white pepper*

yields: ¼ cup

Mash garlic and lemon zest with a mortar and pestle or in a mini-processor. Add the remaining ingredients and combine well. Use immediately.

SUGGESTED USE

whole chicken, rubbed under & over the skin (2 hours)
chicken pieces (2 hours)

Malaysian Paste

4½ tbsp *oyster sauce*
2 tbsp *soy sauce*
1½ tbsp *ketchup*
1½ tbsp *light brown sugar*
2 tbsp *garlic, minced*
1½ tbsp *ginger, minced*
5 small *shallots, minced*
1½ tsp *chili paste with garlic*

yields: ½ cup

Place oyster sauce, soy sauce and ketchup in a small mixing bowl. Add sugar and stir to dissolve the sugar a bit. Stir in the garlic, ginger, shallots and chili paste. Use immediately.

SUGGESTED USE

Whole chicken, or chicken pieces
(1 hour)
pork tenderloin (1 hour)

Moroccan Harissa Paste

3 to 4 *red or green jalapeño chilies, seeded & minced*
2 cloves *garlic, minced*
¼ cup *canned tomatoes, crushed*
1½ tsp *ground cumin*
1½ tsp *ground coriander*
3 tbsp *olive oil*
1 tbsp *lemon juice*
2 to 3 *dried red pepper flakes*

yields: 1½ cup

Combine all ingredients in a food processor and purée as smoothly as possible (it will still be slightly rough in texture). Use immediately or cover tightly and refrigerate up to 1 week or 2 months in the freezer.

SUGGESTED USE

beef steak (1 hour)
pork tenderloin (2 hours)
chicken pieces (2 hours)
whole chicken (3 hours)
shrimp (1 hour)

This paste also works mixed into a mayonnaise or sour cream and used as a garnish or dip.

Mustard Herb Paste

½ cup *Dijon mustard*
2 cloves *garlic, minced*
2 *green onions, minced*
½ tsp *salt*

yields: ½ cup

In a small bowl combine all the ingredients. Use immediately or cover tightly and refrigerate up to 1 week.

SUGGESTED USE

beef steak (1 hour)
pork roast (3 to 4 hours)
pork tenderloin (2 to 3 hours)
chicken pieces (3 to 4 hours)

Mustard Pepper Paste

¼ cup *Dijon mustard*
1 tsp *hot sauce*
½ tsp *dried thyme*
½ tsp *dried oregano*
1 tbsp *black pepper, coarsely ground*

yields: ⅓ cup

Place mustard and hot sauce in a small bowl. Stir together and stir in the thyme, oregano and pepper.

SUGGESTED USE

beef steak (20 to 30 minutes)
pork roast (30 minutes)

Roasted Garlic Paste

4 whole heads *garlic*
¼ cup *olive oil*
1 tsp *salt*

yields: ⅓ cup

Remove excess leaves from the outside of the garlic heads. With a serrated knife cut off the top of each head, exposing the garlic cloves. Place the heads cut side up in a small dish and pour on the olive oil. Cover and roast in the oven at 375°F for 1 hour or until the garlic is very soft and lightly browned. Squeeze the roasted garlic out of the heads and mash with the salt. Keeps for 2 days in the refrigerator.

SUGGESTED USE

beef steak (30 minutes)
seafood or fish (30 minutes)
boneless chicken breasts (30 minutes)

This paste also works well on bread.

Rosemary Mustard Paste

1 clove *garlic, minced*
½ cup *Dijon mustard*
2 tbsp *soy sauce*
1 tbsp *olive oil*
2 tsp *rosemary, chopped*
½ tsp *salt*
¼ tsp *freshly ground pepper*

yields: ½ cup

In a small bowl stir the garlic in the mustard. Whisk in the soy sauce and olive oil. Stir in the rosemary, salt and pepper. Use immediately.

SUGGESTED USE

leg of lamb, with or without bone
(8 to 12 hours)
pork tenderloin (4 hours)

Sambal Mint Paste

2 *serrano chilies, sliced*
½ cup *mint leaves*
½ cup *cilantro leaves*
¼ cup *lemon juice*
¼ cup *cashew pieces*
2 tbsp *vegetable oil*

yields: 1 cup

Place chilies, mint, cilantro, lemon juice and cashews in the food processor and pulse a few times to mince. Then turn on the machine, add vegetable oil and purée. Use immediately or cover tightly and keep refrigerated for up to 1 week.

SUGGESTED USE

shrimp (2 to 3 hours)
chicken breasts (4 to 6 hours)
spareribs (8 hours or more)

Southwestern Paste

2 cloves *garlic, minced*
2 *serrano chilies, minced*
1 tbsp *lime juice*
2 tbsp *paprika*
¼ tsp *ground cumin*
¼ tsp *dried oregano*
¼ tsp *dried thyme*
½ tsp *salt*
2 to 3 tbsp *vegetable oil*

yields: ¼ cup

In a small bowl mash the garlic, chilies and lime juice together to form a paste. Mash in the paprika, cumin, oregano, thyme and salt. Stir in enough oil to make a thick paste. Use immediately or cover tightly and refrigerate up to 2 days.

SUGGESTED USE

fish fillets (30 minutes)
shrimp (30 minutes)
boneless chicken breasts (1 hour)
pork tenderloin (2 hours)

Spicy Paste

2 tbsp *lemon juice*
2 cloves *garlic, minced*
1½ tsp *Tabasco sauce*
1 tsp *chili powder*
½ tsp *ground cumin*
½ tsp *salt*
1 tbsp *olive oil*

yields: ¼ cup

Place lemon juice, garlic, Tabasco, chili powder, cumin, salt and oil in a small bowl. Work together to form a paste.

SUGGESTED USE

shrimp or scallops (1 hour)
pork tenderloin (2 hours)

Sugar & Spice Paste

2 tbsp *garlic, minced*
2 tbsp *kosher salt*
1½ tsp *freshly ground pepper*
⅓ cup *brown sugar*
1 tsp *ground cinnamon*
1 tbsp *dry mustard*
1 tsp *dried thyme*
½ tsp *cayenne pepper*
1 to 2 tbsp *olive oil*

yields: ⅔ cup

Place all ingredients but the oil in a small bowl, and mix together. Add 1 tablespoon oil and mash together. Add more oil to make a thick paste consistency.

SUGGESTED USE

pork loin or tenderloin (30 minutes)

Thai Chili Herb Paste

2 tbsp *soy sauce*
2 tbsp *fish sauce*
2 tbsp *dark brown sugar*
1 or 2 *serrano chilies, minced*
4 cloves *garlic, minced*
3 tbsp *ginger, minced*
⅓ cup *basil, finely chopped*
⅓ cup *mint, finely chopped*
⅓ cup *cilantro, finely chopped*

yields: 1½ cup

Place all ingredients into a food processor and process until it forms a thick purée.

boneless chicken breasts (1 hour)
shrimp (1 hour)
pork tenderloin (1 hour)

Tomato Chili Paste

3 tbsp *tomato paste*
2 tbsp *chili powder*
3 tbsp *water*
1 tbsp *seasoned rice vinegar*
2 cloves *garlic, minced*
½ tsp *salt*

yields: ½ cup

Place all ingredients into a small bowl, and whisk to combine well.

SUGGESTED USE

boneless chicken breasts (1 hour)
pork tenderloin (2 to 4 hours)
pork ribs (2 hours)

Tomato Paste

5 lbs *plum tomatoes*
¼ cup *olive oil*
2 tbsp *olive oil*
to taste *salt*

yields: 1 cup

Roughly chop tomatoes. On high, heat the ¼ cup of the oil in a pan. Add tomatoes and salt, and bring to a boil. Allow to cook for about 8 minutes, stirring until very soft. With a fine food mill, push as much of the tomato pulp through the sieve as possible, leaving the seeds behind. Rub the 2 tbsp of olive oil over a rimmed baking sheet, and then evenly spread the tomato purée. Bake at 300°F, and turn mix with a spatula occasionally. Allow to cook for about 3 hours, or until most of the water evaporates and the surface darkens. Reduce heat to 250°F and cook for an additional 20–25 minutes, until the purée is thick and dark throughout.

SUGGESTED USE

This is a classic tomato paste, that is used in a tomato sauce, beef stroganof, or soup. Store in a jar in the refrigerator for up to two weeks. You can also freeze it for up to 6 months.

Wasabi Paste

1 tbsp *white peppercorns*
1 tbsp *black peppercorns*
1 tbsp *yellow mustard seeds*
1 tsp *wasabi powder*
3 to 4 tsp *warm water*
½ cup *onion, finely minced*
2 tbsp *sake*
2 tbsp *soy sauce*
2 tbsp *mirin*

yields: ½ cup

Place the white and black peppercorns and mustard seeds in a spice grinder or blender and grind to a coarse powder. Stir warm water into wasabi powder until it's smooth, adding more water a bit at a time, if necessary. Let wasabi stand for 10 minutes. Stir wasabi into onions along with ground spices, sake, soy sauce and mirin.

SUGGESTED USE

flank steak or london broil (4 hours)
beef top sirloin (4 hours)
firm fish fillets, swordfish or salmon
(20-30 minutes)

Basting Sauces

Basting sauces are similar to marinades, as they are made for coating meats, fish and vegetables during cooking. Often the food is grilled or barbecued when a basting sauce is involved, but basting sauces are also used when cooking in the oven to provide the meat with moisture, infuse flavor, and allow the outer layer or skin to achieve a crispy texture. Most famously, basting sauce is used for Thanksgiving turkey.

It isn't easy to trace the true history of basting sauce, but it is believed that almost as long as meat has been cooked over a flame or in an oven, someone was inventing delicious sauces to personalize and improve that flavor and texture.

Depending on the meat, fish or vegetable that you are cooking, you will use your basting sauces differently. Generally, however, you will apply it before cooking and toward the end or at the end of cooking. Experimenting with your favorite dishes and also the way you enjoy cooking will help you find the perfect way to use a basting sauce.

Balsamic Basting Sauce

1 cup *olive oil*
¼ cup *balsamic vinegar*
1 tbsp *oregano, minced*
1 tbsp *basil, minced*
1 tbsp *marjoram, minced*
1 tbsp *parsley, minced*
2 cloves *garlic, minced*
1½ tsp *salt*
¾ tsp *black pepper, freshly ground*

yields: 1½ cup

Combine ingredients in a small bowl and whisk together. Store in an airtight container in refrigerator for up to 2 weeks.

SUGGESTED USE

Use this delicious basting sauce with roast vegetables or chicken.

Beef Rib Basting Sauce

¼ cup *cider vinegar*
¼ cup *soy sauce*
¼ cup *water*
¼ cup *Worcestershire sauce*
2 tbsp *paprika*
1 tbsp *chili powder*
1 tbsp *cumin, ground*
½ tbsp *ground oregano*
2 tsp *sugar*
½ tsp *cayenne*
1 tbsp *brown sugar*
1 tbsp *salt*
1 tbsp *black pepper, freshly ground*

yields: 1½ cup

Mix dry ingredients in a glass, plastic, stainless steel or other nonreactive bowl. Add remaining wet ingredients and mix well. Store in the refrigerator in an airtight container. Can be stored for up to one month.

SUGGESTED USE

Apply to your beef ribs before cooking and continue to coat your ribs as you cook. The vinegar in this recipe will ensure moist and delicious meat.

Cranberry Basting Sauce

2 cups *cranberries, fresh or frozen*
1 cup *orange juice*
½ tsp *hot sauce*
½ tsp *freshly ground pepper*

yields: 1 cup

Cook the cranberries with the orange juice over medium heat until cranberries break down, about 15 minutes. Strain through fine sieve and add remaining ingredients.

SUGGESTED USE

whole turkey (30 minutes)
turkey breasts (30 minutes)
whole chicken (30 minutes)

Herb Basting Sauce

3 tbsp *olive oil*
1 tbsp *onion, minced*
1 clove *garlic, crushed*
1 tsp *thyme, dried*
½ tsp *rosemary, dried & crushed*
¼ tsp *sage, ground*
¼ tsp *marjoram, dried*
⅛ tsp *hot pepper sauce*
½ tsp *salt*
½ tsp *black pepper, freshly ground*

yields: ½ cup

Mix ingredients in a glass, plastic, stainless steel or other nonreactive bowl. Use immediately or store in the refrigerator in an airtight container. Can be stored for up to one month.

SUGGESTED USE

Use this basting sauce on chicken breasts by coating the chicken thoroughly and cooking the chicken in the oven, basting occasionally.

Honey Dijon Basting Sauce

3 tbsp *honey*
3 tbsp *dijon mustard*
3 tbsp *soy sauce*
3 cloves *garlic, minced*

yields: ½ cup

Thoroughly mix ingredients together in a medium bowl. Use immediately or store in an airtight container in the refrigerator for up to two weeks.

SUGGESTED USE

Use this basting sauce on pork, by applying before cooking and occasionally while the pork cooks.

Lemon Soy Basting Sauce

½ cup *wine vinegar*
½ cup *lemon juice*
½ cup *olive oil*
1 tbsp *soy sauce*
2 cloves *garlic, minced*
to taste *salt & pepper, ground*

yields: 1½ cup

Combine ingredients in a small bowl and whisk together. Store in an airtight container in refrigerator for up to 2 weeks.

SUGGESTED USE

Brush over just about any meat before cooking, and once again when the meat is done.

Mustard Basting Sauce

1½ tbsp *white-wine vinegar*
1½ tbsp *Dijon mustard*
2 tsp *olive oil*
to taste *salt & pepper*

yields: ¼ cup

Combine ingredients in a small bowl and whisk together. Store in an airtight container in refrigerator for up to 2 weeks.

SUGGESTED USE

Try this with chicken or roast vegetables.

Spicy Maple Basting Sauce

6 tbsp *maple syrup, grade B*
½ cup *water*
2 tbsp *ginger, peeled & minced*
2 cloves *garlic, minced*
1 tsp *dried hot red pepper flakes*
¼ tsp *salt*

yields: ½ cup

Combine ingredients in a saucepan and bring to a boil. Reduce heat to medium-low and simmer until contents reduce to about ½ cup, about 20 minutes. Let cool. Store in an airtight container in refrigerator for up to 2 weeks.

SUGGESTED USE

This is wonderful with a salmon fillet. Cover the salmon and broil.

Soy Basting Sauce

½ cup *chicken broth*
¼ cup *mirin, or rice vinegar*
¼ cup *soy sauce*
2 tbsp *sake*
½ tsp *light brown sugar, packed*
¼ tsp *black pepper, freshly ground*
1 clove *garlic, crushed*
1 *scallion, chopped*
1 1-inch piece *ginger, peeled & sliced*

yields: ½ cup

Place all ingredients in a sauce pan and boil, stirring until sugar dissolves. Reduce heat to medium-low and simmer until contents reduce to about ½ cup, about 20 minutes. Strain through a sieve, and discard solids. Let cool. Store in an airtight container in refrigerator for up to 2 weeks.

SUGGESTED USE

Great for marinating chicken, pork or beef.

Spicy Honey Basting Sauce

¼ cup *lemon juice*
½ tsp *chili paste*
½ cup *honey*
1 clove *garlic, minced*

yields: ½ cup

Place lemon juice and chili paste in a small bowl and stir to dissolve the chili. Stir in the honey and garlic until well blended.

SUGGESTED USE

This will be great with salmon or chicken.

Thanksgiving Basting Sauce

½ cup *melted butter*
1 *lemon's juice & zest*
3 tbsp *Worcestershire sauce*
½ cup *turkey broth*
2 tbsp *chopped fresh sage*

yields: ½ cup

Combine all ingredients in a small saucepan over medium heat, and stir until well combined.

SUGGESTED USE

Great for basting a Thanksgiving turkey.